Inverkeithing and Dalgety
in old picture postcards volume 2

Eric Simpson and George Robertson

European Library ZALTBOMMEL/THE NETHERLANDS

Cover picture: In the top right photograph a *Nelson* class battleship at Ward's Shipbreaking Yard in either 1948 or 1949. The Jubilee Fountain in the High Street (bottom right) was removed shortly after. The mercat cross (centre photograph) was flitted to Bank Street in 1974 to protect it from heavy traffic.

BACK IN TIME

GB ISBN 90 288 2670 x

© 2000 European Library – Zaltbommel/The Netherlands

       Eric Simpson and George Robertson

No part of this book may be reproduced in any form, by print, photoprint, microfilm or any other means, without written permission from the publisher.

European Library
post office box 49
NL – 5300 AA Zaltbommel/The Netherlands
telephone: 0031 418 513144
fax: 0031 418 515515
e-mail:publisher@eurobib.nl

Introduction

In the introduction to volume 1 we summarized the historical development of the parishes of Inverkeithing and Dalgety. Here the emphasis is on the development of the visual record and how it has come to be preserved. The photographic record for our chosen communities is a varied one, and for Inverkeithing, in particular, a rich one, being stretched over a very long period. We are fortunate in that Thomas Keith (1827-1895), one of the pioneer photographers of the Victorian age, visited the auld burgh in the mid-1850s, and photographed buildings like the Gala Tower (see No. 4 and also volume 1) which no longer survive. The pictures of Keith and of other early photographers capture moments in time, moments that have gone and cannot be relived. When Keith, who was an Edinburgh surgeon, came to Inverkeithing, photography out-of-doors was an expensive and complicated procedure. To maximize the light available, Keith's photography was confined to a very short time span, just a few weeks in the height of summer. Any human subjects had to keep absolutely still as the waxed paper process of those days required very long exposures. Accordingly, in the early days most photographs were taken indoors in the studios of the photographic artists, as they liked to call themselves. Their studio portraits of individuals and family groups proved to be very popular. There is no record, so far as we can find, of any studio in Inverkeithing until the 1960s, when first Bill Findlay and then Johnstone Syer (now of Dunfermline) were active in the town. Until then, local people seeking a photographic likeness of themselves and members of their family would have had to go to Dunfermline, Kirkcaldy or Edinburgh for this service.

The invention of the dry plate photograph meant that it was easier to take cameras outside, and both professionals and amateurs took advantage of this new process. One of the amateurs who took outdoor scenes in the Inverkeithing area was Robert Galloway Brand (1872-1941). Educated at Inverkeithing School and Heriot Watt College in Edinburgh, Brand took a number of graphic views of Inverkeithing between 1890 and 1895. In 1992 his local photographs, which are in the form of lantern slides, were donated to Inverkeithing Museum by his daughter Mrs. H. Davies and Nos. 11, 13, and 15 are printed with permission of Fife Council Museums West. A number of Brand's photographs were of Alma Street (e.g. No. 11). It is significant that the 1881 census shows that a Robert Brand, then just ten years old, was living in Alma Street in that year. Brand later moved to Belvedere in Kent where he built his own cinematograph and gave shows of moving pictures at his house. Mrs. Davies, who is a lively 89-year old, tells us that her father, who was an electrician by trade, helped to wire the first lighting system on Blackpool Tower.

In the late 19th century, a number of commercial photographers like James Valentine of Dundee and George Washington Wilson of Aberdeen met the new demand for scenic views and images of streets and historical buildings. Their photographic factories churned out large numbers of photographic prints that could be stuck into a souvenir album. Then, in 1894, picture postcards were introduced to Britain, and within a few years picture postcard production had become big business. Cheap postcards ousted the larger photographic views from the market. To show their friends where they had been, holidaymakers sent off postcards depicting scenes and landmarks on the 'tourist trail' of the day. The High Street, St. Peter's Kirk and the Townhouse with the old mercat cross were among the most popular of the Inverkeithing subjects. Otterston Loch and Donibristle House were just two of the favourite subjects for Dalgety. Proximity to Aberdour, a tourist Mecca, guaranteed a ready sale for the latter subjects. Hillend and St. Davids were also featured. Sadly for us, though, Fordell mining village in the north of Dalgety parish was apparently ignored, although nearby Crossgates and other Fife mining communities were covered. Obviously, too, people liked to send cards depicting the street or area where they lived, so we can locate quite a variety of street scenes for Inverkeithing.

Huge numbers of cards were produced by commercial concerns, some large-scale like Valentine's and others small, often a local chemist's. With postage cheap and more frequent postal deliveries than now, postcards were also utilized to send messages where today we would use the telephone or e-mail. With so many postcards being delivered, many of our Edwardian ancestors became avid collectors. The postcard album collections of the early 1900s sold on to dealers have now become the main source of supply for today's collectors.

For the social historian, artistic works can be a valuable source of evidence. Obviously, before the invention of photography, paintings, prints and maps were the main form of pictorial evidence. One graphic example, illustrated in volume 1, is the painting of the Bonnie Earl of Moray, who was murdered at Donibristle in 1592. Traditional artists, of course, liked to paint picturesque subjects, and the old St. Davids harbour came into that category. The picture reproduced here (No. 59) comes from a book illustration by James Paterson (1854 -1932), a noted Scottish landscape artist. This picture dates back to the time, the start of the last century, when St. Davids was a real working village.

After cheap, simple cameras, like the Kodak Brownie, came into vogue in the early years of the 20th century, simple snapshot photographs became more common. From the standpoint of the social historian, family snapshots are another valuable source of evidence. Not surprisingly, most amateur photographers focused on holiday scenes and places and on family members and friends outside their homes or in their gardens. Sometimes, however, we see people in a work situation, as, for example the snapshots of David Robertson at work at Croftgary Sawmill (No. 53). Occasionally, an amateur, even though possessing just a cheap, simple camera, turned his lens on a subject of more specialist interest, a particular industry or form of transport, for instance. Transport enthusiasts, for example, have helped to preserve for posterity the images of long gone ships and railway engines. Alex Donaldson of Kirkcaldy, for instance, was brought up in Inverkeithing and possessing, as he says, 'only a small simple camera and not much pocket money' took some photographs in the late 1930s which are an invaluable contribution to the local record. See No. 25.

The outbreak of the First World War brought another type of photographer on to the local scene. For their own purposes, for propaganda and official records, the Armed Forces employed professional photographers. During the First World War, images were taken of Donibristle Airfield, showing, for example, hangars and other buildings under construction. Few of these buildings now survive, one intriguing exception being the former photographer's studio which now houses a nursery. A number of images survive too from the Second World War and the immediate post-war period, and a few of these are reproduced here. Some were sent to Eric Simpson by former navymen and women following a press appeal. In those cases some at least of the people shown can be identified. See Nos. 74 and 75.

A number of other images, in the form of old-style glass negatives, were fortuitously resurrected after being discovered hidden in a roof cavity in the former photographer's studio, the present nursery building. The naval men and women shown in these photographs are regrettably still anonymous (No. 72). Bill Prattis, an amateur photographer, who was employed at the Donibristle Royal Aircraft Repair Yard from 1941 to 1959, also took photographs in his place of work. He photographed his fellow employees and sold them prints to help pay for the yard's own magazine. Bill's films had to be developed by the navy's own photographer and passed by the navy's censor. Some of his prints are reproduced here (Nos. 66 and 67), courtesy of Bill himself and of Mrs. O'Donnell who preserved them. Unfortunately, Bill's own archive has not survived.

By this time Donibristle, or Donibee as it was affectionately termed, was under the control of the Royal Navy. But this time, too, we have another type of visual record, in the form of a series of comic cartoons that were painted on a wall in the former Donibristle wardroom (officers' quarters). These cartoons, which take the form of a mural frieze, give a light-hearted view of the life and work of a wartime Fleet Air Arm base and Aircraft Repair Yard. As yet, we have no information as to who the artist was. See Nos. 70 and 71.

Another fortuitous survival is a piece of verse etched on a window pane in a surviving wartime hut (No. 76). It reads:

Dear Friend,
Pause in thy labors for a while,
And offer up a silent humble prayer,
That they who toiled here once but now are gone,
May triumph in the great grim fight,
For life and liberty in the world outside.

This time we have a name attached, namely that of Lieutenant Brian D. Sales, Royal Naval Volunteer Reserve, who added the information that he had been stationed at HMS Merlin (the navy's name for this land-based air station) from March till December 1946. Fortunately, the owners of the hut, Westgarth Auto Services, ensured that when carrying out renovations this precious pane was safely removed. The pane has been donated to Fife Council Museums and, after conservation, will be put on display in Dalgety Bay Library. There it will serve as a memorial to the Donibee servicemen and women, and civilians also, who, during two world wars, helped achieve victory 'in the great grim fight for life and liberty'.

The authors
Eric Simpson is a freelance lecturer and writer. He is a native of Buckie, Banffshire, and has lived in Dalgety Bay since 1966. His books include 'Dalgety Bay – the story of a parish', 'Dalgety Bay – Heritage and Hidden History' (Dalgety Bay Community Council), 'The Auld Grey Toun – Dunfermline in the time of Andrew Carnegie 1835-1919' (Carnegie Dunfermline Trust), 'Discovering Moray, Banff & Nairn' (John Donald), 'Going on Holiday' in Scotland's Past in Action series (National Museums of Scotland), and the script for the video 'Auld Fife' (Forest Edge Films). He is the author, too, of the following European Library publications, namely, 'Aberdour and Burntisland in old picture postcards', 'Buckie in old picture postcards' volumes 1 and 2, and 'Inverkeithing and Dalgety in old picture postcards' volume 1 (with George Hastie).

Eric Simpson and George Robertson have collaborated on four previous European Library publications: 'Dunfermline and Rosyth in old picture postcards' volumes 1 and 2, 'Cowdenbeath in old picture postcards' and 'Limekilns to Culross in old picture postcards'.

George Robertson, a Fifer born and bred, has lived in the Dunfermline area all his life and has had relatives living in Inverkeithing for at least 200 years. He is a former police inspector with Fife Constabulary. At the start of his police service he was stationed in Inverkeithing, based at the former police station (No. 19). Currently employed at the Andrew Carnegie Birthplace and Museum in Dunfermline, he is chairman of Dunfermline Historical Society and is also a voluntary guide for Dunfermline Heritage Trust.

Acknowledgements
We are grateful to those people who loaned material and/or assisted in other ways. While it would be impossible to list every person who helped in one way or another, special thanks must be paid to the following: Morris Allan, Councillor David Arnott, Martin Clark, Robert Cubin, Eddie Deas, Alex Donaldson, David Hamilton, Mrs. Mary Hammond, Rev. George Hastie, Frank Macari, Mrs. Bridget O'Donnell, the late Jane B. Payne, Martin Rogers, Willie Mills, Douglas Murray, W.G. Prattis, Andrew Robertson, Commander Anthony Shaw, Lennox Smith (Sutton Coldfield), G.D Spence (St. Andrews), Bill Wightman (Oxford), Mrs. Janet Willis; also Chris Neale, Penny Maplesden and colleagues at the Carnegie Library, Lin Collis and Lesley Botten of Fife Museums Service, Inverkeithing Local History Society, and Sheila Leahy and Partners in Child Care Nursery, Dalgety Bay. We are also greatly indebted to our wives Kathleen and Maureen for proof-reading and encouragement. For permission to reproduce photographs, we must also thank the Royal Commission on the Ancient and Historical Monuments of Scotland for their generous assistance. If we have inadvertently omitted any names from this list, please accept our apologies.

1   One of the focal events in the Inverkeithing calendar is the centuries-old Lammas Fair. Here we see the crowning of the Lammas Queen in or around 1912. The place is the Square and the buildings are festooned with bunting and flags. The number of spectators, with everyone in their best finery, emphasizes how important an occasion it was. There are two bands present, a pipe band and a brass band. Hats were generally worn in those days and that meant good trade for the milliner's shop shown behind the Queen.

2 At the end of the nineteenth century we are very much in the era of horse-drawn traffic with a gig in the distance coming from the direction of the kirk, a coup cart in the centre of the picture and a wagonette on the right. The wee boys in the Square have their own alternative means of transport, a wooden hurley fitted with old pram wheels. It is summer time and the laddies, although they were wearing uncomfortable Eton collars, went bare fit at that time of year.

3 The left photograph can be dated to the mid-1920s. The A.E.C. charabanc, which was purchased by the Saline Motor Services in 1924, was destroyed by fire in 1927. Motor-driven charas became popular after the First World War, replacing the less comfortable and slower horse-drawn wagonettes of the type shown in the previous picture. Houliston's shop (family grocer and spirit merchant) is now the Ca'dora Fish and Chip Restaurant. In the photograph right we see two 1920s-style vehicles, the van with old acetylene lamps, the car with electric headlights. Comparing this photograph with No. 1, we observe that the shop facing south has been drastically altered. It now has dormer windows, larger shop windows, and a new façade, but the central door pillars have been removed as the premises have been divided.

4   Going back in time again to the late nineteenth century, we note that R.J. Cunningham's grocery shop has small paned windows, not the plate glass which became fashionable in the following century. The tall building, the Gala Tower, is illustrated in volume 1, but here we see it from a different angle. The forestairs on the dwellings on the right were later removed, possibly at the same time as the Gala Tower itself, which was demolished around 1890. Note that some of the roofs were pantiled and that the street and pavement appear to be hard packed earth. The street gutters, however, were lined with causey setts. With so many quarries in the area, there were a lot of settmakers in Inverkeithing.

5 This is another of Inverkeithing's historic buildings, which stood on the High Street close to the Gala Tower. It survived at least until the early 1920s. In this building William Roxburgh was born. Like Admiral Greig, he was a Royal Navy officer who transferred to the Russian navy and served with such distinction that in 1776 he was promoted to the rank of Rear Admiral. The presence of a cycle depot is an indication of how popular cycling had become since the introduction of the safety bicycle in the 1880s. The notice on the drain pipe reads: 'Royal Enfield Cycles.'

(Crown Copyright: Royal Commission on the Ancient & Historical Monuments of Scotland.)

6 This group of historic buildings (top photograph) dates back to 1937. The lane on the left was popularly known as Bible Raw, so called because some of the residents had once been noted for their strong evangelical bent. Note the gas street lamp. The corbie-stepped buildings were demolished in 1962. The building with the distinctive forestairs (numbers 95 to 99) was located at the south end of the High Street. There is a new building here now with two shops on the ground floor. Alex Hutt, whose premises are on the right, was not just an ordinary baker. As he proclaims on the shop front, he is a pastry baker and confectioner. There is still a baker's business, Bayne's, on the site.

(Crown Copyright: Royal Commission on the Ancient & Historical Monuments of Scotland.)

7 Bottom photograph: almost opposite we find an ironmongery store at 62 High Street, with Adam Waugh himself standing at the doorway. Judging by the cleverly arranged window displays, provided by the manufacturers, he seemed to have specialized in paints and radio. Radios in those days, the 1930s, required large dry batteries: observe the adverts for Exide and Drydex batteries and what looks to be a rechargeable glass accumulator battery. Other items sold included vacuum cleaners, crockery and razor blades.

8   Providence House with its door lintel dated 1688 is at the northeast corner of the square and is seen here, right, in 1937. Despite the position of the garage sign, the building was not used for this purpose. Blair's garage was adjacent. Facing the camera and wearing a waistcoat is Norman Macari, proprietor of the shop behind which sold fish and chips and icecream. Norman Macari, who was born in Falkirk of Italian parentage, did military service in Italy in the 1920s, then later joined the Black Watch but during the Second World War served in the Royal Air Force. On the left picture we have a slightly later image with the shop boasting a new sign above the door, with Norman Macari, still waistcoated, in the centre with family and friends around him.
(Crown Copyright: Royal Commission on the Ancient & Historical Monuments of Scotland.)

9   Port Street, formerly identified as Shore Wynd or Sea Wynd, was once an important thoroughfare, since it was the only street that led directly to the harbour. After the railway line from Dunfermline to North Queensferry was built, circa 1877, it lost its importance, since access to the burgh's port and commercial heart was provided by a new street, Commercial Road. Obviously, the footbridge across the railway was of no use for vehicular traffic. Observe the street well and surface gutter, both common features throughout the burgh at one time. The photograph was taken just prior to demolition of the houses shown on the left side.

10 This milliner's shop stood in King Street, close to Port Street. Judging by the cloche style of hats in the windows, the date is late 1920s or early 1930s. Wearing hats was then de rigueur, so milliners did good trade in those days. The proprietor, though, wears a dress that belongs to an earlier era. The premises were later used as a barber's shop. King Street, incidentally, was formerly known as the Mill Raw. This picture was evidently taken off a glass negative, which, as we see from the top right corner, had been broken.

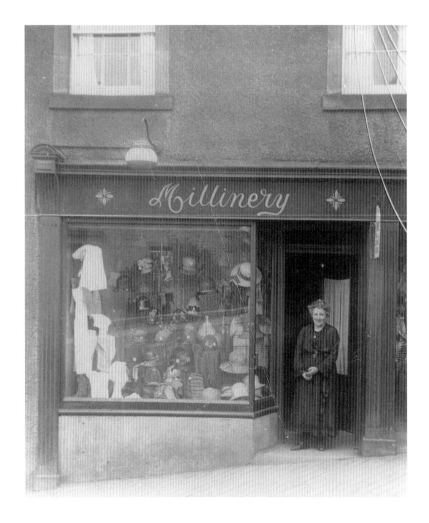

11 Now we proceed to the lower end of Alma Street photographed by Robert Brand in 1895 (see Introduction). Again there is a street well at the top of the road. All the houses on the left, with the exception of the topmost one, have been replaced. The trees at the top have gone and been replaced with the dwellings of Elgin Park. The pavement (on one side only) and street surfaces leave a lot to be desired. The well-dressed gentleman is holding a child's wooden wheelbarrow. Gowk Hall and Court Gait were old names for this thoroughfare, the street being renamed after the Crimean War victory in 1854.

12 The name of Waggon Road, illustrated here, derives from the early waggonway or railway which passed along it towards Inverkeithing harbour. The track had been part of the Halbeath Railway which was opened in 1783 and carried coal from the Halbeath pits until 1867. This stretch of the Halbeath line shown here survived well into the 20th century. The houses have all gone. Between their site and the now also demolished Distillery stand the Maltings, a recently constructed block of flats.
(Crown Copyright: Royal Commission on the Ancient & Historical Monuments of Scotland.)

13 The track of the Halbeath Railway appears again on the left of this circa 1890 Robert Brand photograph which was taken from the Boreland Brig. The tracks on the right were constructed for the old Dunfermline to North Queensferry Railway with a branch link to the Halbeath line. The same tracks were later utilized for the rail link to Rosyth Dockyard. Note the goods station, which had its own platform, on the right. In the centre we see the Keithing Burn with a lade going off on the right to serve the water mill, which was at the foot of King Street. There was a mill here at least as far back as the 13th century. In 1850 a steam engine (note the big chimney) was installed to provide an alternative source of power. At the time this photograph was taken the mill was no longer in use. The tall building on the other side of the burn (to the left of the mill lum) had also been a mill, but in 1884 had been converted into a tenement. All these structures have now disappeared.

14 The main railway station was opened when the Forth Railway Bridge was completed in 1890. Previously there was no direct connection between Inverkeithing and Burntisland. The buildings on the left have now gone and a new station building erected in 1985. The waiting room on the right has been greatly altered. Also gone are the telegraph poles, the weighing machine on the platform, the gas lamps and the wooden fence. The adverts too have altered. In the year 2000 a new footbridge, which allows disabled access, was added.

15   The Halbeath line comes into view again just to the right of the Keithing Burn and looking north to the Inverkeithing Fire Brick and Gas Retort Works at Burnside. This plant, built around 1831 by James McVicar, was steam-powered and would have been supplied with coal via the Halbeath Railway. As McVicar went bankrupt, the business was rouped in 1843. The buildings shown here included kilns, drying sheds and stores. In the 1860s, nineteen men were employed there. It closed, circa 1895, around the time when this photograph was taken by Robert Brand. After closure, some of the buildings were converted into dwelling houses. Doubtless, some of the chimney cans and bricks manufactured there survive to this day in and around Inverkeithing.

16 Scots Mill shown here is now in ruins, but it was another of the historic mills of the district. It stood to the west of Hillend and was supplied with water by a lade taken off the Keithing Burn. The grain-drying kiln with its roof vent is on the right. Because of the risk of fire, kilns had iron floors. The remains of the metal pegs which supported this floor are still visible. Since the water from the wooden trough has been diverted into the cast, it is evident that the mill was not being worked at the time of the photographer's visit. Water mills generally could be used for different func-tions, but we know that in 1855 it was a flour mill. The mill closed in 1913.

SCOTS MILL, INVERKEITHING.

J. R. B.

17 Here the water mill is on the left. As the mill of Caldsyde, it dates back at least to 1528. The name Scotsmill comes from the Scott family who were the 16th century owners of Caldsyde. The pantiled-roofed cottage was the miller's house. Though it was a neat looking building, this dwelling is now also a ruin. The lady in the door-way and the reclining gent are both wearing straw boaters. This dates the photograph to the early 1900s. The mill name is commemorated as Scotmill Way in Inverkeithing (to the east of the railway sta-tion) and as Scots Mill Place in Hillend (one of the new streets at the west end).

18 Here we have (right) the fish shop of Henry S. Murray photographed in the late 1930s or 1940s. In the picture we see John McKay, then Charlotte Cunningham, and Sam Hardy. Henry Murray himself is peering through the window. The corrugated iron building was erected in the early 1920s. Observe the telephone number, 84, which digits still feature in the firm's current number.

Younger son Willie continued the business after his father died in 1963. Ten years earlier, elder brother Jim had taken over the other two shops (see the 1970 image on the left) and operated them as a newsagent's and grocery. The shops were demolished to make way for houses. Jim Murray also ran shops in North Queensferry and Dalgety Bay (now the Bay Stores).

He was a prominent figure in local affairs, being involved in many kinds of voluntary work including chieftainship of the Inverkeithing Highland Games. A grandson of Henry Murray continues as a fish merchant in Inverkeithing to this day.

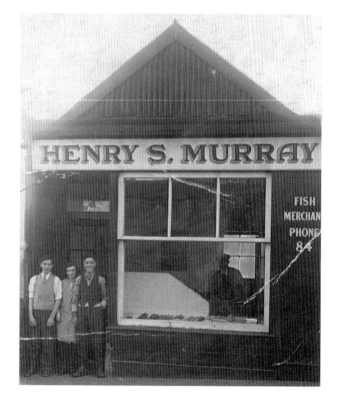

19   Now we turn to Roods Road, circa 1928, where the police station was once situated. The door on the left gave access to the police office and cells at the back of the building. Sergeant McLaren shown here occupied the ground floor of the house to the right, and a constable the upper storey. Sergeant McLaren was a weel kent figure in the town, being in charge of the local constabulary from 1925 until his retiral in 1935. He came back to the police during the Second World War to help out because of manpower shortage. On the right we see Mrs. McLaren and on the other side daughter Janet (now Mrs. Willis.) Mrs. Willis can recall having to answer the telephone when the officers were out on patrol, and particularly during the difficult period of the 1926 General Strike. George Robertson, co-author, started his police career at this station. Except for the railings removed for scrap during the Second World War, the buildings still stand but have been converted into private dwellings.

20 In volume 1, a photograph appears of Thomas and David Steedmans' Hillbank Smiddy circa 1910. This time we show their former premises in Abbot Place off Hope Street. This photograph and advert probably just predate their move to Hillbank. The blacksmiths are posed in front of their pantile-roofed smiddy, each holding one of the tools of their trade. There were no fewer than eleven blacksmiths listed in the 1910/11 Business Directory for Inverkeithing. As their advert states, the Steedmans made and repaired, in addition to the usual agricultural implements, railings and gates. Repairing and sharpening lawnmowers was another speciality. Possibly, too, they did work for Donald Laird, posting master at the Queen's Hotel stables, Inverkeithing. His advert displays a horse-drawn brake.

21   Here we have another of the burgh's industrial sites, the gasworks of the Inverkeithing Gas Company off Waggon Road to the south of King Street. The time is the 1890s and we see yet another stretch of the Halbeath Railway. This time, however, we see one of the horse-drawn coal waggons used on the line. There appear to be two horses here pulling in line. Immediately behind the waggon we see, at the back of the dyke, the framework for the circular gas holder which appears to be empty. The 1925 Ordnance Survey Map shows a very much enlarged gas works which survived until the advent of North Sea gas. The field behind is now occupied by the houses and gardens of Spittalfield Crescent.

22 Spittalfield Road, illustrated here, is an example of the first council houses built in the early 1920s after the Addison Act of 1919, a landmark measure in the history of municipal housing. The design is typical of council housing of that period, with either four or two dwellings per block. When this photograph was taken, the street was incomplete and Spittalfield Crescent had yet to be built. Beyond the last block on the left appears the substantial building called at that time the White House Hotel. A tannery stood on this site till the early 1900s. The name Spittalfield, the Rev.

William Stephen tells us, means the field of the hospital, or hospice, of the Queensferry Passage. To the east of Spittalfield Road, we see the embankment for a short railway line which ran between the former Donibristle Airfield and East Ness Pier. Fraser Avenue now occupies the land in the foreground.

SPITTALFIELD, INVERKEITHING.

23 To the left, in the foreground are the dwellings which were created from the former ropeworks which, as we can see from this pre-1914 postcard, extended a considerable distance to the east. Other industrial sites include the paper mill with its big lum and adjacent shipyard. Since Inverkeithing was never an important fishing port, a major puzzle is the presence in the bay of over thirty fishing boats. The vessels are Fifies, sailing drifters, which probably came from the East Neuk ports. Maybe they had been laid up there at the end of the herring season, or else they had been engaged in sprat fishing. The boats are lying on land which was then tidal, but has since been reclaimed to create the Ballast Bank recreational area.

24 In this circa 1900 view, we see the East Harbour, as it was once named, which was constructed at the mouth of the Keithing Burn. The pier on the right, the former Mid Pier, carries a railway line which gave access to the main line and was used for industrial purposes, as we can see from the coal hoist at the end of the pier. The two sailing ships on the right are cargo vessels, possibly colliers or some other kind of coastal traders. Goods brought into Inverkeithing included esparto grass, woodpulp, starch, and china clay. Cruicks Quarry, on the far shore, was opened in 1828, and has been greatly enlarged since this photograph was taken.

25 Preston Quarry, on the other hand, was opened in the latter half of the 19th century and is now closed. Whinstone was carried to the lofty jetty shown in this 1930s snapshot (left). The ship taking on stone was a 'Firth' coaster of the Fisher Line. At that time a Mr. Donald Clark was the quarry manager. Returning to the main harbour for the other photograph, we see, on the right, two steamships, the nearer being the *Elizabeth Bromley* and behind her the *Rosie*. These small coasters transported esparto grass from ocean-going ships across the firth from Granton to Inverkeithing. The lighter on the left was used for the same purpose as circumstances required. This area, now filled in, was formerly known as the West Harbour.

26 The *Rosie* appears again in a mid-1930s view (left), but this time in the East Harbour. On the right we see two railway waggons and, on the Ballast Bank, we have a funfair with stalls, merry-go-round, and caravans. In the other photograph, we look across the East Harbour to Caldwell's Paper Mill, an establishment notable for pioneering the manufacture of greaseproof paper in this country. The railway waggons are on the former Mid Pier. There had been an earlier pulp mill, but the Paper Mill as such dates back to 1892.

27   In this dramatic view of 24 May 1913, we see the end of the old Caldwell's mill. The mill at that time was largely built of wood. The fire destroyed not just the mill and associated buildings but also the machinery. Reconstruction started immediately, with the mill being built of brick this time. Operations were resumed in the following year. Ironically, that very day a large crowd had left Inverkeithing for Glasgow to see Inverkeithing Juniors play in the Final of the Scottish Junior Cup. The attendance was 20,000 and Inverkeithing beat Dunipace by one goal to nil.

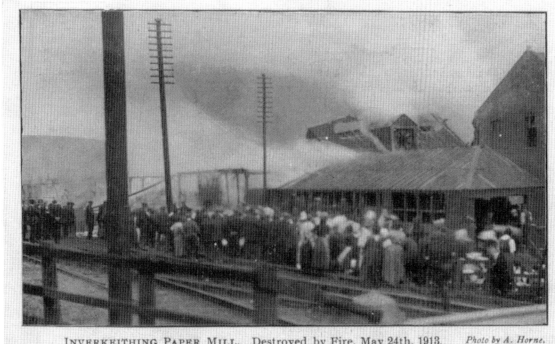

INVERKEITHING PAPER MILL. Destroyed by Fire, May 24th, 1913.   *Photo by A. Horne.*

28 Now we turn to the interior of the Paper Mill around 1930. We see in this department how labour-intensive sorting and packaging could be. Except for two men (both wearing bunnets!), all the employees are female. The women are tidily dressed and the younger ones coiffured with the then fashionable bob cut. The design of the mill was greatly admired by papermakers who came from far and near to study the layout.

29 Some of the ladies from Caldwell's Paper Mill appear also in this early 1950s image. Obviously the girl in the handcart is the bride to be. For her wedding send-off, her colleagues have presented her with a cake, dressed her up and decorated the cart, which just possibly was borrowed from the mill itself. Everyone is dressed for this very special occasion. Two of the women are wearing turbans, a style of head dress which came into vogue during the Second World War. Were, though, the wee boys meant to be there? Certainly they appear to have been tidied up for the occasion.

30 This advertisement for the shipbreaking yard then known as Ward's shows the *Implacable*, a fleet aircraft carrier moored ready for breaking. This 26,125 ton ship had a distinguished war record, taking part, for instance, in the Pacific campaign. Surplus to requirements after the war, she was broken up at Inverkeithing in 1955. Many other famous wartime vessels were also broken up at Wards, including the battleships *Rodney* (1948) and *Nelson* (1949) and liners like the *Empress of Australia* (1952) and the *Mauretania* (1965). Also broken up were ships of local interest: the Forth ferryboats *Queen Margaret* and *Mary Queen of Scots* and the coaster mentioned in No. 25, the *Elizabeth Bromley* in 1960.

SHIPS DISMANTLING BY WARDS

Many thousand tons of valuable scrap, recovered from such ships as the aircraft carrier H.M.S. 'Implacable' (pictured) are sent to the foundries, helping to satisfy the continual demand for steel. Our yards have been 'last berth' to famous ships—H.M.S. 'Royal Sovereign', 'Nelson', 'Formidable', 'Rodney'; merchant vessels 'Empress of Australia', 'Llandovery Castle' among many others.

THOS. W. WARD LTD
THE BAY - INVERKEITHING

PHONE: 460   GRAMS: 'FORWARD, INVERKEITHING'
HEAD OFFICE: ALBION WORKS · · SHEFFIELD

31 Ward's was an extremely busy yard when on 15 May 1954 Morris Allan, a Dunfermline commercial photographer, took this aerial view. Three large vessels are being broken up, the middle one of the three could be the hulk of the aircraft carrier *Formidable*. Two large merchant vessels are also tied up, awaiting disposal. The larger one is a big liner, the other probably a cargo liner. To the east, we see some of Inverkeithing's early council housing schemes. While there is as yet no Spencerfield Road nor Barr Crescent, the road for the, yet to be constructed, Fraser Avenue is just visible.

32   Leaving Inverkeithing we come to Seggsburn on one of the roads leading to North Queensferry. This row of thirteen houses was built in the late 1890s. The postcard was posted in 1909 about ten years after completion and the caption seems to indicate that at that time they were owned by Fife County Council. The cottages were reputed to have been built on a bog, but had no sanitation! The Seggsburn row had to be demolished in 1962 to make way for the approach roads for the Forth Road Bridge.

County Council Cottages, Inverkeithing.

33 This early 20th-century postcard now brings us to North Queensferry, a village with a long history as a ferry station. In the stage coach days the inns were busy establishments. Since change horses were often required, each stage coach inn needed commodious stables. The stables for the Albert Hotel were housed in the L-shaped building, which we can see at the water's edge, bottom right. Once railway services became established, the stage coach became redundant. For some years this now superfluous stable block served as headquarters for a rowing club and afterwards as a store for a local joiner. The building no longer exists.

Forth Bridge.

34 Now we turn to North Queensferry's Main Street (left) as viewed in the early 20th century. The Free Church on the left was opened in 1878 and demolished in the early 1960s. Note in front of it the Great War memorial, which now stands on the opposite side of the street. Next door we have the Roxburgh Arms, now the Ferrybridge Hotel. The proprietor's name as given in this card is M.I. Hislop.

Nearby we see Niven's butcher's shop in the mid-1920s. The proprietors also farmed at Ferry Barns Farm, another property demolished to make way for the Forth Road Bridge. Other members of the Niven family owned butcher's shops in Inverkeithing and Aberdour. The shop girls in the doorway are the Brown sisters. Observe the laddie wearing knickerbockers.

Church and War Memorial, North Queensferry.

35 The tall building, left of centre, featured in this early 20th century scene (top photograph) was locally known as the Matchbox House for obvious reasons. It was demolished in the 1970s. Also gone are the cottages on the extreme right. These were temporary wooden dwellings erected for men employed on the construction of the railway bridge. Afterwards they were occupied by bridge maintenance workers. The huts were later replaced by buildings of a permanent nature. The site is now occupied by a car park. The other postcard dates back to the same time. Note the washhouses on the left, built against the wall of St. James' Chapel. Observe too the old street pump on the left. The early 19th century houses on the right were replaced in the 1970s.

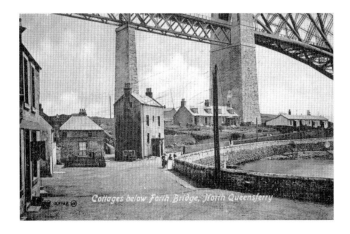

Cottages below Forth Bridge, North Queensferry

Chapel Close, North Queensferry

36 North Queensferry station was opened when the railway bridge was completed in 1890. This picture was taken not long after. The photographer had positioned himself above the exit from the railway tunnel. The big lum beyond the station poses a problem. Perhaps it was part of the Carlingnose Farm complex. To the east we see Carlingnose (carlin means a witch). On this promontory we see a coastal defence emplacement erected at the beginning of the 20th century. When the First World War broke out in 1914, the Carlingnose battery, with its two six-inch guns, was incorporated into a system of defence lines, designed to protect the warships anchored in the Forth. Later in the war, the main defence line was shifted eastward, so Carlingnose was disarmed in 1916. The nearby Coastguard battery with its two 12-pounder guns was, however, retained. The barracks were subsequently used by Royal Engineers and Territorial Army troops until sold in the 1960s.

CARLIN NOSE, NORTH QUEENSFERRY.

37   During the First World War, North Queensferry, like all the neighbouring Forth communities, saw a considerable degree of military and naval involvement. Above, we see a site under preparation for the construction of a kite balloon station. On the left side of the picture, we see the line of the former Dunfermline to North Queensferry Railway opened in 1877 (see also No.13). The date of this photograph is 12 February 1917. A few months later we see the completed station with the naval officers and staff being inspected by the Commander in Chief. These huge tents housed kite balloons which were used by the Royal Navy for spotting enemy ships. The balloons were towed by destroyers searching for U-boats. The approaches to the Forth Road Bridge now cover this site.

KITE BALLOON STATION, N. QUEENSFERRY.
VIEW OF KITE BALLOON STATION LOOKING SOUTH.   12-2-17

KITE BALLOON STATION, N. QUEENSFERRY.
VIEW OF OFFICERS & STAFF.   4-5-17

38 Another type of balloon is featured in this illustration, this time a barrage balloon of Second World War vintage. These hydrogen gas-filled balloons were flown to protect places and structures of military and strategic importance such as Rosyth Dockyard, Donibristle Airfield and warships anchored by the Forth Railway Bridge. This balloon was anchored at Carlingnose. Part of the barracks mentioned in No. 36 can be seen, top left. The vehicle to which this particular balloon was attached is a Bedford truck, known as a Prime Mover. This vehicle was used to float a balloon or move it from one site to another. In all there were twenty barrage balloon sites around North Queensferry, Inverkeithing and Donibristle. The crews were provided by the RAF and later also by Polish Air Force personnel, who had managed to escape the German occupation of their country.

39 Here, top, we have a Bedford Prime Mover but this time at Seggsburn. We see a corner of one of the Seggsburn cottages in the background (see No. 32). The Bedford lorry is in a strange position because it had been dragged from its normal stance by a runaway balloon during a winter gale. Part of the deflated balloon appears, caught in the trees, top right. The date is 1940. RAF officers and crew are inspecting the damage. The postcard below shows an artist's impression of the first German air raid on the British mainland on 16 October 1939. The German bombers were attacking, not the Forth Bridge as is commonly believed, but naval vessels in the Firth of Forth. The British casualties of the raid are buried in the military section of Douglasbank cemetery. It was as a result of this aerial attack that the barrage balloons of 948 Squadron were moved north to the Forth area.

THE FIRST NAZI AIR RAID ON SCOTLAND 16TH OCTOBER 1939 WHEN OUR GUNS & FIGHTER
PLANES ENGAGED THE RAIDERS, DROVE THEM OFF, & BROUGHT SEVERAL DOWN.
THE FORTH BRIDGE WAS UNDAMAGED.

— COPYRIGHT —
CAITHNESS BROS
KIRKCALDY.

40   Right, we have the front cover for a 1957 booklet listing toll charges and conditions of carriage for the historic Forth ferry crossing. The toll charge list includes hand barrows, perambulators, and a variety of animals including cows, oxen, sows, sheep, and goats. Curiously, a stallion was charged more than three times the cost for a mare or gelding. Likewise, it was far more expensive to transport a bull than a cow. A hearse was charged 9/6d but, if it was carrying a corpse, a further 12/6d was added. However, as we can see from the photograph taken at the south side, the ferries in the 1950s were transporting motor vehicles rather than animals. The booklet gives the names of the four ferry boats in service at that time, all names of national figures. The list had to include *Queen Margaret* since the ferry passage, the 'Passagium de Inverkethin', was started at her behest to carry pilgrims heading to St. Andrews.

" Queen Margaret," " Robert the Bruce,"
" Mary Queen of Scots " and " Sir William Wallace "

Queensferry Passage
FERRY
FOR THE CONVEYANCE OF
ALL FORMS OF TRAFFIC
PASSENGER & VEHICULAR

BETWEEN

North and South Queensferry

Telephone—
South Queensferry
No. 253

Manager: R. A. MASON
Hawes Pier
South Queensferry

Workers of the Ferry:
William Denny & Brothers Ltd.

March 1957

41 Now we are at the North Queensferry side of the Forth. It is the early 1900s and a few well-dressed spectators are watching the chauffeur-driven car being driven off the boat. Very few cars were carried in those days and the *Forfarshire*, built in 1861, was not designed for that purpose. In 1893 the Queensferry Passage was leased to John Wilson of Bo'ness who purchased this former Tay ferryboat, which remained in service for over twenty years. When not engaged on her regular sailings, the paddle steamer carried sightseers on excursions to see the marvellous new bridge across the Firth of Forth. In this picture we see her tied up at the Railway Pier, which was built to serve the Dunfermline to Queensferry Railway.

42   Having now arrived at Hillend, we are looking eastward along Main Street towards the Hillend Tavern. Note the telegraph poles. With no pavement on the north side, the mud scrapers at the first two doorways would have been in constant use. In 1893 a sanitary inspector drew attention to the insanitary condition of the village, there being no drainage system and only a very limited supply of water. The village was split between two parishes, the west end belonging to Inverkeithing and the east to Dalgety. It was at this end that the school for Dalgety parish was located. The Hillend school was closed in 1970.

43 Here now is Hillend, viewed from the east end. The post office, with the lamp attached, is on the left. Incidentally, part of the bracket is still attached. The doorway beneath the lamp has been blocked off and has been replaced by a window. There are several horse-drawn vehicles visible but no motor cars. In the automobile age, before the bypass was built, Hillend Main Street was a very busy thoroughfare.

Hillend, Inverkeithing.

44 In the early 1970s, when this photograph was taken, there were no fewer than three petrol filling stations at Hillend. Two of them were at the west end. Forsyth's service station and garage is shown here at the east side. Quite a number of the early residents of Dalgety Bay had their cars serviced there. The car park for Dalgety Bay railway halt now occupies this site. Notice how bare the south side of the road is compared with today.

45　At the north end of Dalgety parish, we come to another village, Crossgates, which straddles three parishes, Beath to the north, Dunfermline to the west and Dalgety to the southeast. Springhill, left picture, came into Dalgety parish. In this circa 1900 postcard, we note that the bairns were free to play on the road. No danger of fast moving traffic in those days! Many of the single-storey cottages were occupied by coal miners, the village being in the centre of a busy mining area. In the illustration right, we see one of these dwellings, part of which has been converted into a shop. The date is around 1921. The owner, we are told, was a Mrs. Beveridge and the shop sold, in addition to the usual sweeties and groceries, tallow wax and wicks for miners' lamps.

Springhill looking East Crossgates Fife.

46 We are still in the Crossgates area, outside Mossgreen Parish Church. This kirk had been erected in 1852 to cater for the growing mining population in the area from Fordell to Crossgates. These images were copied from glass transparencies supplied by Lizars of Edinburgh. The occasion is the unveiling of Mossgreen War Memorial and the date is 21 May 1920. The unveiling was performed by the Laird of Fordell, the Earl of Buckinghamshire and his daughter, Lady Dorothy. The guard of honour was provided by men from Donibristle RAF Station. Note in the right hand photograph the bugler sounding the Last Post. Two bands were present, the pipe band as shown and the RAF brass band from Donibristle. Seventy-eight names are listed on this First World War memorial, thirty of them from the local Black Watch regiment. Although the kirk has gone, this memorial to the fallen still stands.

47 Fordell House is another historic building that has disappeared. It was photographed in 1963 just before it was demolished. It was built in 1721 by the Henderson family, who owned the Fordell coal pits and the dwellings of Fordell village. This mansion was meant to replace Fordell Castle as the family residence. Ironically the castle, which has been restored, still survives. The site of the house has been cleared and trees now grow where the garden was situated and the house stood.
(Crown Copyright: Royal Commission on the Ancient & Historical Monuments of Scotland.)

48 The main part of Donibristle House, when photographed in the early 1900s by George Washington Wilson, was obviously a ruin (left picture). The block shown here, built in the early 1700s, had been gutted by fire in 1858. The site was cleared in 1912, but the side pavilions (see No. 49) survived the fire. In the left picture, we are looking southward towards the Firth of Forth. In the right view, we now look at the house from the opposite direction. As we can see from the drive, the carriage entrance is on the east side. An entirely new building, in mock Georgian style, now occupies the site. Unlike the original, which was the main residence of successive Earls of Moray, its modern replacement is a flatted block.

Ruins, Donibristle Park.

Donibristle Castle (after second Fire), Aberdour.

49   This time Donibristle House is viewed from the east. This allows us to see the wings which survived the 1858 fire. The postmark on this Valentine's card is 1943. Since, however, the main house is also visible, the photograph must be pre-1912. Valentine's had slipped up with this postcard, as that firm usually blotted out features which dated their cards. From 1939 to 1976, the two wings were occupied by high-ranking naval officers. In 1984, after a period as a sales office, the west pavilion was gutted by fire. The buildings and the ornamental railings, which separated the two blocks, were reconstructed by Muir Homes Ltd. in the 1990s.

50 Donibristle Estate covered an extensive area. There were two principal entrances, one, still in existence, in Aberdour opposite the Woodside Hotel. Here we see the former West Gate which was situated at the north end of the road leading to Regents Way from the A921. The gate with its ornamental surrounds was removed in 1964. The wrought ironwork was then flitted to the Earl of Moray's estate at Darnaway in Moray. The man with the horse-drawn vehicle is presumably an estate employee. The whole structure is evidently meant to impress visitors and onlookers alike.

51 There were quite a few dwellings for estate workers, including several lodges. Here we have the former West Lodge which appears on the left side of the previous illustration. Both photographs can probably be dated to the late 19th century. Again we clearly see that the lodge, built to house a humble estate employee, was at least externally a prestigious building. Observe the pelican on the portico, a heraldic device which appeared also on the ironwork of the gate and side pillars. The 1891 census tells us that the Donibristle West Lodge was occupied by a Janet Matthewson. The occupation of this 80-year old was given as gate keeper. The elderly lady standing between the pillars is, in all probability, Janet herself. The only other occupant was her 18-year old granddaughter, Jessie, who was a pupil teacher.

52   St. Colme Cottage, on the shore, just south of St. Colme House, was another estate house. Observe the diamond-paned windows and the rustic style architecture, a complete contrast to the classical or Georgian design of the West Lodge. For Mrs. Mary Hammond, who went to live there in 1941, it was 'her little bit of heaven', despite there being no electricity and no road to it. When her furniture was delivered, it had to be flitted across the fields by tractor and trailer. Coal was delivered by wheelbarrow. The imposing gateway to Dalgety Gardens (photo below) was another Georgian structure. Though the gateway was demolished to make way for new houses, part of the walls survive, protecting the present-day street which perpetuates the name of Dalgety Gardens.

53 The Earl of Moray's estates in this area comprised a number of farms and other enterprises. Dalgety Bay, except for St. Davids, is largely contained within the former Donibristle Estate. Adjoining it to the east and north was the earl's Cullaloe Estate. Croftgary Sawmill and cottage (left picture) were included in the latter, but the sawmill did work for both estates. The sawmill is just over the border in Aberdour parish and was mainly powered by water from the Dour Burn. The sawmill, which is the lower of the two buildings, dates back at least to 1854. The picture right shows David Robertson, father of Andrew, the present occupant. When it was still a working sawmill, sawing stobs, fence rails and gates was a major part of their work. After the Cullaoe Estate was broken up in 1951, Andrew Robertson purchased the sawmill and adjacent cottage and still resides there.

54 Returning to Dalgety parish, we arrive now at Otterston Loch. In the postcard (left), Valentine's were trying to convey the impression of an artist's palette and brushes, with the loch framed in the centre. Looking to the north, we see on the left Otterston House which was demolished circa 1950. On the extreme right, we see the ruined Couston Castle which was restored by Dunfermline businessman, Alastair Harper, in the 1980s. The lochside cottages behind the castle still survive. Right we have a 1930s snapshot of the loch in full winter guise. While some people are skating and a few playing at ice hockey, most are just walking on the ice. The scene is almost reminiscent of a Lowrie painting.

55 The former manse for the parish of Dalgety was completed in 1830 to serve the new kirk built that same year. (That kirk building is now occupied by the congregation of the Cornerstone Full Gospel Church.) The manse, designed by James Gillespie Graham, was conveniently placed, just east of Barns Farm and close to the new kirk. The manse was built on the church glebe. In 1897 a fire in the manse led to the loss of a large proportion of the kirk session records, a serious loss from the standpoint of local historians. Also destroyed were two fine mid-17th century silver communion cups. After 1940, when the parish of Dalgety was united with Aberdour, Dalgety manse was sold and it is now a private residence. When in 1965 a separate Dalgety parish was reconstituted, a new manse had therefore to be built.

56 In 1976 oil giants Shell and Esso decided to use Braefoot Bay as a liquid gas tanker terminal, linked to their gas separation plant at Mossmorran near Cowdenbeath. This caused alarm among the residents of Dalgety Bay and Aberdour. In view of the potential hazard and loss of amenity, a protest campaign was launched. Part of the protest action involved a gathering in June 1977 at St. Bridget's Kirk where locals, dressed up for the occasion, demonstrated their concern. 'Shell-Go' is the slogan on the banner. The late Nicholas Fairbairn, M.P., is on the extreme right. The campaign, however, failed and the project went ahead, since it was deemed to be in the national economic interest.

57　When the central block of Donibristle House was demolished in 1912 (see No. 48), the space cleared was converted into a cricket pitch. This was probably done during the time (1939-1976) when the Admiralty rented the two surviving wings. The roof of the east wing is just visible. The little pavilion on the right was demolished for the later Muir Homes development. In 1978, when this photograph was taken, Dalgety Cricket Club took up where the navy left off and played their home matches on this beautiful pitch. When redevelopment plans for the area were brought forward, the club had to go elsewhere. In 1989 Muir Homes Ltd. purchased the site and some years later commenced building the houses which now occupy this ground.

58 The Mills family occupies a cottage that survives from the days of the Moray Estate. Willie Mills used to farm fields which were later built over as the town expanded. As their farm land was gradually diminished, the family diversified by establishing a fruit and vegetable shop, which was based in sheds adjacent to their dwelling, which was the former gardener's cottage. Here, Mrs. Mills is inside the shed serving one of their many local customers. The family provided a very good and welcome service to the local community, until the supermarket in the main shopping centre became established. This photograph was taken on 4 November 1988. The business was closed the following day.

59   St. Davids was a busy but bonnie little seaport as we see from this painting by James Paterson. It was so picturesque that publishers T.N. Foulis selected the painting as one of the illustrations for Stewart Dick's book 'The Pageant of the Forth' (1911). Paterson, who was a noted artist in his day, specialized in landscapes in oil and water colour. The artist had positioned himself on the west pier, looking across to the main east pier where the shipping agent's office and house were located. These buildings were roofed with red pantiles. In depicting the harbour scene, the artist had the luxury of being able to indulge in a degree of artistic licence.

60　Now we are looking westward towards St. Davids with Letham Hill behind. The harbour with village was founded in 1752 by Sir Robert Henderson of Fordell for the purpose of exporting coal from his pits. The Fordell Railway was later constructed for the easier carriage of his coal from the north of the parish to the harbour. At the extreme left of the pier we see the hoists which were used to drop coal from the railway waggons to the colliers below. The most prominent of the buildings on the pier housed the shipping agent's dwelling and office.

61 In the early 20th century, the steam yacht *Crystal* was a frequent visitor to St. Davids, her owners being the Earl and Countess of Buckinghamshire. The Countess was descended from the Hendersons of Fordell and her husband had become the laird. A former resident of the village recalls that the villagers were expected to show due deference to their superiors. When the Earl and Countess arrived in their own private railway carriage and walked down to their yacht, the women curtsied and the men doffed their caps. One wonders what the Earl and Countess of that day would have thought if they had known that their trim little village and seaport would finish up as a maritime scrapyard.

62   On 3rd August 1950 the Fife Free Press reported that the village was due to be demolished as soon as new homes could be found for its forty inhabitants. This decision had been taken on the recommendation of Fife County Council's Medical Officer, because of the total lack of lighting, water and sanitary provision. A closing order was applied to all the houses, except the Customs House and a house adjoining the hotel. The former building, as we see from the photograph, had been left high and dry in the middle of White's shipbreaking yard. As its name indicates, this building had served as the Customs House when foreign vessels were a common sight in the harbour. It was demolished when the scrapyard site was cleared in the early 1980s.

63 Another of the St. Davids buildings, which survived into the 1950s, was the Fordell Arms Hotel. It remained open for a short period although the rest of the dwellings were derelict. This advertisement appeared in the Donibristle Repair Yard Magazine No. 2 of November 1950. It is a clever advert with several deliberate puns, since the term Gee can be interpreted in several different ways. The presence of the cartoon aircraft points to one possible aeronautical explanation, namely a reference to a radio-navigational system of that time. The Fordell Arms had long been a local howff for the Donibristle aerodrome personnel. As we note from the second illustration, the Woodside Hotel at Aberdour was another favoured location for social activity. We don't know when exactly this 'select' dance was held, but it was sometime during the Second World War.

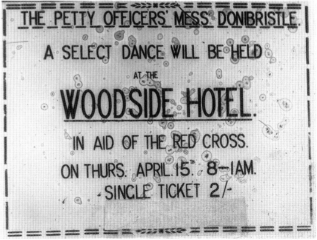

64 In the 1920s and '30s, Donibristle aerodrome, or Donibee as it was popularly termed, was an RAF base. On the right picture we see staff, both civilian and military, who served the officers' mess in the early 1930s. Janet McLaren (now Mrs. Willis) is third on the left. Mrs. Willis, a lively 88-year old, was a civilian cook at the mess for three years. She had, she recalls, very little contact with the RAF officers whom she served, although there were occasions when she had to stay overnight to prepare meals, if a flight was due very early or late. She left when, in October 1935, the airfield was placed on a care and maintenance basis. With war an imminent threat, it was soon fully operational again. The postcard left reflects the change that had taken place, when in May 1939 RAF Station, Donibristle, was closed down and was immediately transformed into the Royal Naval Air Station, Donibristle. The navy named their new base H.M.S. *Merlin*. The aircraft shown in this Christmas card are prewar torpedo bombers.

65   During and after the Second World War, Donibristle Airfield housed both a Royal Naval Aircraft Repair Yard and the Fleet Air Arm base, H.M.S. *Merlin*. On the previous page we see the emblem for H.M.S. *Merlin*, and now we have on the right the badge of the repair yard. The Donibristle yard made a major contribution to the war effort, with the staff, both men and women, often working day and night to equip and repair naval aircraft urgently required for major operations. By 1944 some 2,000 civilians and 1,000 servicemen and women were employed at the yard. While the airfield, operated by the Fleet Air Arm, was closed in 1953, the yard survived until 1959. On the left picture, looking west towards Letham Hill, is the airfield with its control tower and main runway. The photograph was taken in 1965 by Lennox Smith, who had returned to see the place where, from 1946 to 1947, he had spent time as a National Serviceman. These buildings were demolished soon after.

66 Here we see some of the repair and maintenance hangars and some of the civilian workers with a Grumman Wildcat. The photograph was taken in April 1945, while the war was still being waged. This aircraft was an American-built fleet fighter bomber. It could carry a 200lb bomb and was armed with six 0.5 inch machine guns. Initially, the Royal Navy gave its own name to it, calling it the Martlet. As the Fleet Air Arm's first single seat monoplane fighter, it was a decided improvement on the Sea Gladiator, its biplane predecessor. Commander Shaw (see No. 69) described it as a dinky little fighter.

67 This photograph, like the previous one, was taken by W.G. Prattis. Bill, an Inverkeithing man, had started at the Donibristle yard in 1941 and was one of the earliest of the local civilians to be employed there. Photography was his hobby and, rather unusually, he was permitted to photograph the work of the yard. Some of his images were reproduced in the aircraft yard's magazine. However, all his pictures, including the two used in this book, had to be censored, and also developed by naval personnel. The plane is a Wildcat and here we note how vitally important women were to the war effort.

68 The yard repaired and serviced aircraft which had to be tested and then delivered to air stations all over the United Kingdom. It was the pilots from the ferry pool, illustrated here, who performed these duties. The officer on the left is Sub Lieutenant George D. Spence, who served as a ferry pilot at H.M.S. *Merlin* in the late summer of 1944. All the pilots are Royal Navy, except for one, third from the right, who is in the Air Transport Auxiliary. Note that the officers wearing jackets, unlike their RAF colleagues, wear their wings on their left sleeves. The Royal Navy balked at any form of ostentatious display, preferring that pilots' wings be displayed as inconspicuously as possible. They had to be on the left sleeve, as badges on the right would be too prominently exhibited when saluting! As may be seen, this regulation did not apply to battle dress tops. The plane is a Seafire, the naval version of the Spitfire.

69   Midshipman Shaw was another young pilot who had joined the Donibristle ferry pool two years earlier. He also delivered planes to bases from Orkney right down to the south coast. It was great experience, he says, flying so many different types of aircraft and having to cope with bad weather. Since radar communication for air traffic was then at a rudimentary stage, you had to find your own way. Fortunately, he tells us, the country was littered with airfields and, in extreme circumstances, you could often land and enquire as to your whereabouts. Later he flew a Seafire from a carrier to give ground support for the 1943 Salerno landings. The following year, while again on ground attack duties, he was shot down in the South of France. Captured by the Germans, he made a daring escape, was recaptured and escaped again, this time successfully. We see him here as a young R.N.V.R. officer standing by a Spitfire. After serving for 33 years, he retired with the rank of Commander and now resides in Dalgety Bay.

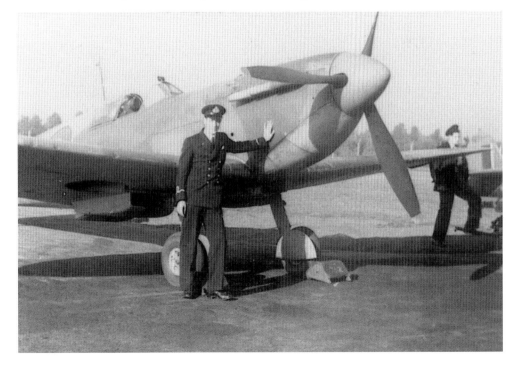

70 Now we turn to the wardroom (naval parlance for officers' mess) where officers like Commander Shaw were accommodated. This satirical cartoon forms part of a frieze in a small room within the former Donibristle wardroom. When it was painted no one can say for sure. It was probably not there in the Commander's time, as he has no recollection of it. The artist depicts wartime navymen in mock Ancient Egyptian style of dress. The squad on the right are engaged in target practice under the eagle eye of a ferocious looking Petty Officer. While one naval policeman heats his kipper at the stove, his colleague uses a candle to warm his toes. (Crown Copyright: Royal Commission on the Ancient & Historical Monuments of Scotland.)

71 Here we have a more extensive view of the frieze and how the various segments reflect different aspects of the life and work of a 1940s naval air station. The section above the fireplace shows a board meeting with a senior officer presiding while his clerks hammer out the minutes using mallet and chisel. The joke is compounded by having a mock coat of arms underneath. One mystery remains. Who was responsible for this remarkable piece of work? The existence and survival of this frieze at least demonstrates that the station commander had a sense of humour. The building was later incorporated into an electronics factory. At present, the factory stands empty and its fate, and that of the frieze, remains uncertain.
(Crown Copyright: Royal Commission on the Ancient & Historical Monuments of Scotland.)

72   On the left, we have a group of top brass, led by a Rear Admiral, arriving at Donibee for some kind of inspection. We don't know who they are, but observe the 'scrambled egg' on their caps and their well bulled shoes. Prior to their arrival, some of the ratings would have been hard at work whitewashing the marker posts. On the right is a contrasting group, six anonymous ratings, date circa 1943, rather obviously not on parade. They are the people who did the donkey work, servicing, repairing and refitting the navy's aircraft, like the Swordfish that they are leaning against. The Swordfish was a biplane torpedo bomber, which, though slow and out of date, proved a very effective weapon in sea battles like the one in 1941 that sunk the German battleship the *Bismarck*.

73 The plane here is a Mark XV Seafire, a complete contrast to the Swordfish. This plane, number SW917, was built in 1945. It had crashed in early 1947, while on a test flight, and here it is being retrieved by the Donibristle salvage unit. Lennox Smith, who worked on her, kept records detailing her repair costs, which were £1,669: 15 shillings and 2 pence. What the twopence was for remains a mystery. The Seafire, pilots say, was a beautiful aeroplane to fly. It, however, had disadvantages as a deck landing aircraft, namely its high landing speed and lack of robustness.

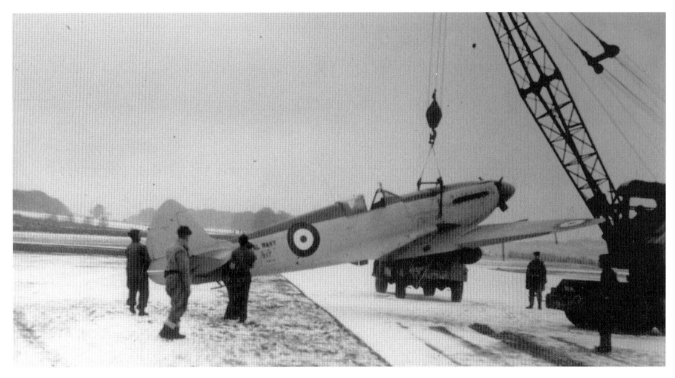

74 When planes crashed, the fire tender was quickly on the scene. This crash tender, photographed in April 1946, is manned by aircraft handlers led by Leading Seaman Les Potter on the left, who was de-mobbed the following day. He was succeeded by Leading Rate Bill Wightman, who is second from the right, in the front. Bill, who provided this photograph, served at Donibee from 1946 to 1947. In the harsh winter of 1947, he tells us, airfield hands were shovelling snow off the runway every day. Bill was treated to a flight on a number of occasions, ground crew being fitted in if there was spare room in one of the planes. The Flag Officer Air in his time was the Macintosh of Macintosh, a Rear Admiral. Bill's tender had to rush to his house on one occasion: for a chip pan fire!

75 Now we have a dramatic scene with a Seafire, which has crashlanded and is on fire. However, this is actually a training exercise. The Repair Yard supplied the fire crew with old aircraft which were set on fire with a dummy in the cockpit. In this photo we see Bill Wightman on top of the plane, hauling the 'pilot' out of the cockpit. This was no easy matter, Bill tells us, since the dummy, which was made from asbestos, weighed ten stones. The crew's standard issue steel helmets and Wellington boots seem pretty basic.

76 It is appropriate to finish with this unique memento of the old Donibee airfield and repair yard. This is the inscription referred to in the introduction. The pane has been preserved and the intention is that, after conservation, it will be displayed in Dalgety Bay Library as a memorial to everyone who served at the airfield and yard and who thus helped to preserve 'life and liberty'. To conclude we repeat the verse:

Dear friend,
Pause in thy labors for a while,
And offer up a silent humble prayer,
That they who toiled here once but now are gone,
May triumph in the great grim fight,
For life and liberty in the world outside.

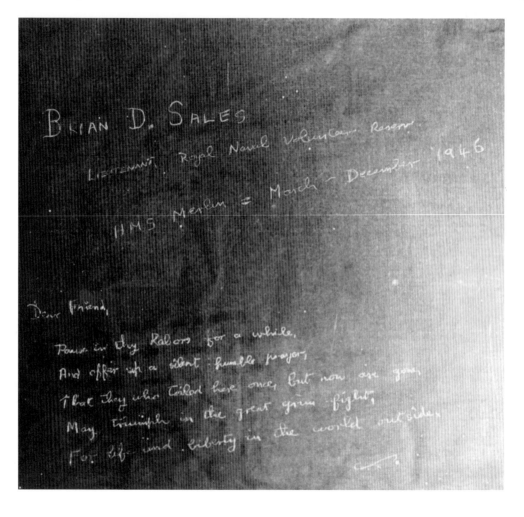